Valparaiso

MARY O'MALLEY was born in Connemara, educated at the National University of Ireland, Galway. She taught for eight years in Lisbon, where her children were born. She was an organiser of the Cuirt Festival in Galway for eight years and has served on the board of Poetry Ireland. She taught on the MA in Writing and the MA in Arts Administration at Galway University for several years, and has been active in environmental education for over twenty years. She was Writer in Residence at NUI Galway from 2001 to 2009, and has held residencies, at the Centre Culturel Irlandais in Paris, in Derry and in Belfast, the latter involving working with traditional musicians, and with the classical music organisation Music for Galway.

Mary O'Malley is a regular broadcaster on the Irish national radio station RTE I, and travels regularly to the United States and Europe to write and lecture. Half of *Valparaiso* was written in Paris, where she spends time every year. She is a member of Aosdána, and has received Hennessey and O'Shaughnessey Awards for her poetry.

T0099115

Also by Mary O'Malley from Carcanet Press

The Boning Hall
A Perfect V

Three Irish Poets: Paula Meehan, Mary O'Malley, Eavan Boland,
edited by Eavan Boland

MARY O'MALLEY

Valparaiso

CARCANET

First published in Great Britain in 2012 by

Carcanet Press Limited
Alliance House
Cross Street
Manchester M2 7AQ

www.carcanet.co.uk

A CIP catalogue record for this book is available from the British Library

ISBN 978 1 84777 135 3

The publisher acknowledges financial assistance from Arts Council England

Supported by
ARTS COUNCIL
ENGLAND

Typeset by XL Publishing Services, Tiverton
Printed and bound in England by SRP Ltd, Exeter

Tháinig long ó Valparaíso.
Scaoileadh téad a seol sa chuan.
Chuir a h-ainm dom i gcuimhne
Ríocht na gréine, tír na mbua.

'Gluais,' ar sí 'ar thuras fada
liom ó scamall is ó cheo.
Tá faoi shleasaibh ghorm Andes
Cathair scáthmhar, glée mar sheod.'...

Padhraic de Brun

Came a ship from Valparaiso
Dropped her anchor in the bay
Her name was magic and a praisesong
To the red-gold kingdom far away.

'Go,' she said, 'on your long journey
Away from misery, rain and cold
Below the knife slash of the Andes
There's a shining city, shaded, jewelled.' ...

Mary O'Malley

Acknowledgements

Special thanks to the Irish Marine Institute, the Master and crew of the *Celtic Explorer* and to the Arts Council and the Centre Culturel Irlandais in Paris.

Thanks to the editors of the following magazines and programmes where some of the poems in this collection have previously been published or broadcast: *The Cork Literary Review, Fusion Magazine, Hibernia Review, The Irish Times, Ploughshares, Poetry Ireland Review, The Recorder, Southword, Temenos Academy Review,* RTE Radio 1, CD for Connemara Sea Week.

Contents

I

Poem on a Leaf	11
The Way	12
At Jardin des Plantes	13
Antikythera	15
Coda	16
Dido, Grainne, Brid	17
Recession Eve	18
Mystical Things	19
Philoctatea	20
In the Seminary	21
Entropy	22
The Lost Boys	23
Two Heads in a Landscape	24
Instress in Ireland	25
Mercy	26
The White City	27
The Lisbon Bride	28
Israel	29
Last Night in Paris	30
The Guide	31
Still Life	32
Whom the Gods Love	33
One Year On	34

II   Resident at Sea

I	Sea Road, No Map	37
II	Oceano Nox	40
III	Abyss	42
IV	Shore	44
V	Narthex	45

III

Veteris Vestigia Flammae	49
More Space than Stars	50

Play It Again, Sam   51
Homage   52
Before Winter Comes   53
Faith   55
Dreampoem I   56
Dreampoem II   56
Interregnum   57
Civet   58
Watching the Stuttering Lovers   59
If   60
An Easement for the Chest   61
Instead of a Proposal   62
No   63
Tesseract   64
Manchester   65
Coelacanth   66

IV

The Lusiads   69
Ekphrasis   70
The Myth of Language   71
Crew   72
Thalassa   73
Neap   74
The Shark's Dream   75
Caged   76
Cetorhinus maximus   77
The Black Glacier   78
To All Who Are Hopeless with Birds   79
Statues   80
Caravaggio's Hands   81
Homesick   82
The Birth of Venus   83
Climbing the Volcano   84
The Gulls at Fastnet   85
Never Merely One Albertine   87

Notes   88

I

Those who go on voyages seldom come back holy.
Thomas à Kempis

Poem on a Leaf

for Kevin

Be life veined
Be strong as winter.
Be the sun's dance
On every water.

The Way

Out now, the years gone up in smoke
the firebird in ashes. It's time.
The sun is rolling up the slope,

a thousand people rang the fire brigade last night.
A five year old was shot, children are burning.
I could write many verses to stop this flight

the packed red suitcase, the light's pewter slant
on the water. And have. But back to leaving. I am.
The ice blue nights, the carapace of wit

hidden like some mermaid's cap.
Leaving the jewelled women, the men like cattle
heavy, smug. No plans, just a cheap

flight to some mythic city called Hotel
or Airport. There are no countries left
only the deep territories, the blackened hills.

At night we miss our countries and whisper secretly
how we loved their fragile borders,
their lakes, their fields too green for mercy.

You'll go to the interior, and choose your mountain.
I'll take the coast.
How strange setting out in the world again.

I hear the earth is not reliable, the poles
not where they ought to be. I never thought they would,
but wanted stamps, and rest among the pilgrim souls

all maps discarded, just the studded way of paintings
signposted in shells, the hope of travellers' courtesy
and all our road unravelling before us.

At Jardin des Plantes

The sea begins where the story has broken
and it is richer than heaven
especially in mid-ocean

where creatures like pearls hang
dead spheres, eggs without shells.
They are preyed on by few

in their spectral world. Once a globe
of blue pulsed down faster than war
rare as a monk shinning down a rope.

Inside the diving bell a man
who might have saved or loved them
saw nothing. His blindness became wisdom

and they were left alone for years
until curious Frenchmen turned
their journeying minds

to the pelagic, the profound
region and saw that those milky creatures
shy as spectres in the diver's arc

have one talent, which is repulsing light
to save themselves
from notice and from death.

Decades before, whole schools
on rue St Jacques and in the Marais
became empty plaques

because pearl children failed
to escape detection when Picasso
and all France closed their eyes to avoid

the light that shone on Max Jacob
and Irène Némirovsky and found them luminous
in those penumbric times. Discovered

what the twilight creatures knew until
they too were investigated and turned
into exhibits to make us flinch or marvel

at what we manage not to notice
until it is presented tagged and dead
a story on a glued vase, in jagged pieces.

Antikythera

He hung over the side a cigarette discarded
a chain with its crucified Christ
flashing in the sun, and blessed himself.
His breath opened O and again O
took in the whole element and time
and all the sub-atomic particles,
took them into his chest and dived.

He found the old half-rotted star clock
all bronze and green and verdigris, then
he saw the women coming at him like ghosts
falling towards him out of the wreck
with their strange virginity, and dropped it.
By the time he reached the surface
he was gabbling, they said, about bodies

said it with their kind's terror of superstition.
Flattened like an old watch dumped
its secret stayed buried in a lost codex
long after the pearl diver found it,
teeth at an angle, grinning at the moon.
Then they got it all wrong and squabbled
like bankers over their interpretations.

They say its clock was set at Libra
which may mean nothing
though blind chance did not design the cogs,
chance, or some rival fleet, sank the ship.
Scientists computed, disputed its purpose
but it was into the sponge diver's arms
the beautiful dead women fell.

It was he found the treasure
because he was down there among the old irons,
old bottles, poking around where it all starts
with the sea-crazed   star-hungry   sea-crossed.

Coda

The sea is a language scientists parse
sentences of current and wave.
Fishermen speak it, sing it, curse
its dynamics when it raves.

Dido, Grainne, Brid

Some believe you do not choose the myth
it fastens to you at birth and come the day,
you recognise it, own or deny
as here in a room in the Fifth
where priests were made
and unmade she enters, Dido
from the river, to help.

                Her trick
of getting territory not through marriage,
but with bull's hide and mathematical brilliance
reminds me of Brid, our spring saint,
our virgin politician and that Grainne
who saddled power and broke it,
had the man, the child, the grief and did not,
that we know of, complain.

Recession Eve

Ban teabags. Grow your own
oranges and chocolate. Divine
the limestone for the best wine.

Take up knitting and learn to stitch. Good luck.
It's deadly dull, though you could knit
yourself a new man or assemble one quick

enough from Chinese barbecue instructions
with missing bits, a leg sticking out like an elbow
and wonky logic, just like the old malediction.

He would fix the roof, protect you from storms
and in an ideal world, while you knit a garden
with a tree in blossom, unblock the drains.

Then forgetting the heartache, the dropped stitches
you'd eat the apple out of his hand again
and spin gold from the serpent's promises.

Mystical Things

Wars and worse. Mantillas, headscarves
male and female bicycles.
Add churching, sex
mortal, venial and reserved
and you have our miserable childhood
in a soundbite
though not four angels round my head
not the rose on the pillow
not the old dried blood on the wall.

Is it different in India? At night
Ghandi had two virgins to test his purity.
He was old then, dear old skin and bones.
Two virgins just like St Scrotius. For God's sake
why not whiskey and cake?

Philoctatea

In each new city you pray to fling down your crutches.
It never happens, even here with the Eiffel Tower
sparkling like a panther's necklace and the Dior police
with their eager truncheons. You think you can still riot?
You, hobbling along on your understated crutches
under the protection of lipstick and Sainte Chapelle – such blue!
– and your ruined foot in your green iguana shoes?

In the Seminary

I sleep fitfully. Last night I dreamed myself
in the arms of one man, woke to the care
of a cold lover, old friend. This comfort, so rare
in my convent state, makes me rash. What if?

Faith. Why not? Buy a blue silk skirt on Rue Princesse
put it on and head out along the drunken river
to meet destiny or death, a trace of cognac on his lips.
How do you like your green-eyed girl now, Mister?

Entropy

It's been half a lifetime but I've tried.
I called, I phoned, I e-mailed

and besides the odd sign and one
ten-fingered miracle, no word from you.

I'm fine. If you're there you'll know
that lies like this are venial so

how about yourself? Things fall apart.
I might be talking to myself but faith

unfashionably dies hard as hope
so I thought this telegram might work

being urgent and old-fashioned
and you so out of favour, Lord.

The Lost Boys

Like old action men, their limbs askew
from too much bashing, their knotted faces
stare at the sky when they are put out
on the city dump for recycling
                              the lost boys.

They are plastic, indestructible.
When their world breaks into splinters, each piece
reflects jaggedly. At best this mosaic hurts the eye
and the soul snags on it. (The soul is not plastic.)
This is what they long for, the lost boys:

                              the sun to fall
into the lake and, silvered, become moon
mirror, whole again in which the other's face
eyes, heart are seen as in a game of divination
at Hallowe'en. The heart with their name.

                              Instead a hand
holds a cup, china, delicate, walking across a minefield.
On her finger a jade ring. Her warm smell is missing.
One hand, one cup, tea gleaming like honey
in the mirror's shattered eye.

Two Heads in a Landscape

after Goya

They have no cities here and starve for want of one
whose swan castigates God, one black exiled angel
beating for his dead love, as the spinster sister wheels
towards France like a lost plane, her brothers flown

from Lough Derravaragh, with women of their own.
We choose our fate in those double-ended stories.
Out of the rubble, the rows of tinpot houses,
the new ghettos, from the bottom of endless potholes,

the moon laughs at them, cityless.
Only the scrap tower, honest coinage, gleams.
The changing heart is a two-dimensioned house
and they lie silently in its thin shelter, pitiless

as a kicked dog howls and whimpers. They wake
to the tin carousel of the next morning and the next,
which we call lucky. They wanted more,
that sin, original, and still the best. Love, of sorts.

Instress in Ireland

on the publication of the Ryan Report

From ibi to illic the *road up down one* is paved
with muons, pions, men in cassocks,
seeds of blight in a child's iris deflected
distorted, trodden down when all the soul
requires is a champagne glass
brimming with claritas

and sweet neutrinos passing through
leaving such faint traces
driving through our teeming nights. All this time
they were passing through us like ghosts
about their own purposes
silent as grace, the glorious mysteries.

O Plato, Scottus, Ignatius with your rotted stalks
we should have turfed you out years before this.

Mercy

We got our Christianity from Egypt, not Rome
But the Pope won
So all the convent girls sing oh oh oh
De Bello, Bello Gallico.

The White City

i.m. John O'Donoghue

is the one we carry with us. Its walls shield
us from the salt wind. In the discalced lanes,
people with occupied faces stream along
about their business and do not regard you
with suspicion. Perhaps they recognise you
as one returned after a lifetime away in places
where orderly crowds flow only towards graves.

A man your age is being buried today.
A million hands are raised to strike
at children, or worse. A million fingers
move along their lovers' cheeks,
stretching away to infinity like powers of ten.
There are millions left for mopping up

and to click keyboards by the blue light
of absolute stupidity. There are perhaps
twenty generals brilliant with ambition
and sex waiting in the wings.
The white city pulses in the sun,
wanton as May, ordered as the moon.

There are cafés, a rented room, the comfort
of strangers. Bright scarves trail like adjectives
along the waterfront. The man I summon
speaks of the Tao and a Jesuit education.
Nothing really happens there or here he says,
but time passes. It passes through us and tells me
he wants to live to be old, to know how it feels.

The Lisbon Bride

It floats in on an imaginary horizon seeping light,
its slender bridge, and the old rose streets
restored every few hundred years.
After the great fire, lilies and carnations – snow white

rose red – explode in recompense. There is safety
in cities built on earthquake lines.
You know where you stand, if not exactly
when it will all explode and the surprising thing is

mostly it doesn't, underpinned as it is by lament,
so much less brittle than joy. Peacocks scream
like political prisoners, their cries shivering out
over the walls in hot daylight. They are rare, white.

A girl newly arrived in Seteais calls for tea
imperious as all brides. The marriage will not work.
When she enters the city this time she will pity
their love, the cracks already spreading, the aftershocks.

Israel

It's me. Talking to you after all this time
driven out to the green limit of the firs to ask
before the bright absence flows again,
an empty armful of light glistening,
why you sent the devil my way
his fur singed by coals, so early.

He drove me into the arms of the angel
in every way more dangerous
and this horse I was condemned to ride,
his red tongue, his teeth open like the jaws of death
rides me. Have you no pity?

Last Night in Paris

after Dulce María Loynaz

Here are my delights – I believe there are none
missing. Light them like candles.
Speak them with your lips.

Here are my sorrows – they are at my heels,
obedient and you have your own pack.
How well we have trained them.

Before I walked away I did not explain:
this is who I am. Now take my sorrows
and burn them. Spread their ashes in your garden.

Let me lie on your heart.
I have nowhere to go
and without them I am light as a swallow.

The Guide

He said, if there is somewhere else after this
somewhere the dead live outside of memory –
I cannot think it is much of a life for them
in our memory and for what it's worth I
would like to know they populate the endless suns –
that elsewhere is no consolation for the salt tang
and the green water nor for skin
though perhaps it is a cure for pain.

Perhaps. All this reeling backwards (he said)
to when skeletons were girls and wrecks were ships
loading at quays for voyages is exhausting
so just weigh anchor in the car or at the desk
and pray death comes when we are not looking
and steals us away from our untidy houses.

Still Life

All that is left is a woman slicing lemons,
crushing thyme. Silence has reefs
of absent voices to be avoided as heroes
steer clear of sirens. I might do this myself

if I could believe the will finds its own pace
that most things, even the curse loneliness
lays on us resolve themselves
but the fish's eyes are full of tears.

All that is left is the lemon, the table, the blade
which gleams, dull as old scales. Outside
someone is standing at the window
sharpening his eyes.

Whom the Gods Love

Hessian on her fingers, his skin a fever
of burning membrane,
she dries down her swan lover,

washes the oil, black on black, off his feathers
with suds, wearing rubber gloves,
her touch crudely human. The air shivers

and parts. The swan ambulance
vees in, skates water. Zeus' doctors
are here with their stethoscopes.

He rests on the down stretcher. Someone else
has taken over. She falls back. The swan ambulance
takes off like an arrow, wheels once

on white wings over the sick town, bends
upwards and he's gone. Left, she takes off her gloves.
There is tar on her wrist. It's like that, the end.

One Year On

i.m. Mark Joyce

To commemorate you
the paper birch
a blue-band jug
such an ordinary vessel
for a song
I have no heart to sing.

A spill of notes along the lakeshore.
This at least is.
A triangulation,
safe from the crude definition
of simple sums,
the exact dimensions
of the suit of sails made in Boston
for the Aran gleoiteog,
might point us where you went.

Let it hold
all that cannot safely be loosed
in the refrain
at its end and its beginning,
the O of birth,
the last surprised breath.

II
RESIDENT AT SEA

Da molte stele mi vien questa luce
Dante

I *Sea Road, No Map*

I said to you I will die if I stay
And you said Jesus we'll die anyway.
You spoke as if I did not exist.

What world would have me? A ship.
She moves me on from impossible Ireland,
the wrack of ties I have knotted
too tightly, things I do not understand
like gardens, sisters, why days
taste flat. We slide out the bay, past Salthill
leaving Galway rampant,
the drug dealers, the scrap merchants,

a city at the races, every horse wild eyed,
the merchant class handing one another rosettes,
flanks heaving at how well we are doing
under the lash. Under the last arch
three musketeers raise their cans
to another new hotel – how many new hotels
can the homeless need?
The Buckfast kids under the bridge
will start no revolution

the guns are moving in another direction
and gunmen have to make a living somehow.
Cliffs, birds, Blaskets slip by. I think
can we keep on going to Valparaiso
and never come back. Surely it will be easy
in Valparaiso, with oranges and tin hearts
and only one kind of fruit,
and no voice following
with one half of a conversation.

It was making day when I looked out
at the kind of beauty
that leaves death unthinkable,
purple slate, gannets rising in small explosions

and everything makes sense.
The world is round again and we are its sun
describing a horizon, ratskin waves stretch to America
lumps of sea rise under the bow and below
acres of drowned Ireland and a mountain.

The sea is streaming through him.
His eyes dissolving in salt water, sting.

Is this how the soul might know itself
fathoming, like two saints meeting

on the way from Rome,
one saying this is a flowering plain

picking a bluebell and offering his proof archly
the other saying this is the sea

and scooping up a salmon in reply
fathoming deeper intentions

small treacheries
the slant pitch of the deck

forcing the centre inward
somewhere near the solar plexus.

Today, he'd be fined for the sea's bounty.

I am dissolving.
What would sing in me is the deep ocean

the roll and pitch of her voice
the wrecks, fish, instruments

the drowned and those who swim in her.
Land makes sense

from this distance, we hear
its jangled music like a score.

We shift destination to Nymph's Bank.
Dinophysis lures the scientists
now inland, now offshore
now, unexpectedly, to the sea-floor.
Inside this small hub all is domestic
and office. Computers, phones, faxes
link us to land, to our houses
to the hand on the phone

(there is no hand on the phone)
in the hall, a kitchen in Donegal
a living room in Brest.
We wash our cups make snacks, watch
the progress of the deluge in England.
A young spaniel is swimming through the streets
and even this triumph of endless rain
results in comedy and grief.

The washing machine hums, someone coughs.
Helena is working out in the gym.
Miles away Ireland
is rich in tribunal and gridlock.

II *Oceano Nox*

'In the midst of the sea there is a horned island
with deep green harbours where Greek ships anchor'...
Derek Walcott, 'Omeros'

Awake at four, the moon,
a headache, stabilisers rumbling
I know instantly where I am.
Below us are old Greek instruments
for calculating the influence of the stars;
now it is all geometry again
the nun's harsh voice
is ionann an cearnog ar an teoragain...
first lessons in the sweet art of navigation

and everything, the stars' measured light
the toxic red tide, flown, snatched at
as in a dream pulsing
with its own diurnal rhythm.
What's drowned in the sea is buried in the cortex,
an X-ray of all the lost possibilities
the things we know, bunches of violets
silvering a line and things we don't,
the deadly run-off from a mine.

The sea swings her skirt indifferently.
A red tide gathers in a thin horizontal column.
Her mate is the hard bed
from which she is drawn.
Creatures fine as glass ride her thermals –
the caped dinoflagellates –
swivelling jewels the colour of peridots,
and dinophysis, the scientists' prey
red, handsome, bad.

Ghost nets waltz along the bottom
fishing. They catch shark, whales.
They snatch music from the dead
whose bones make perfect instruments –

the sternal notch from a drowned soprano,
(in life her slight vibrato might have marred
Rusalka's aria), an ivory Jew's harp
from some rough sailor
the delicate wantbone of an ex-nun.

All night I hear them practising in tune
a pale choir caught in monofilament.
In the poisoned bright of nudiebacks,
seaslugs. The dull gleam of a chalice *Pai*
afaste de mim esse cálice, Pai
or in the shrouded limbo of the pelagic,
the abyssal water, where creatures
with strange sexual habits reproduce
there are works buried in the mud.

Antikythera, rare as the Mona Lisa
your wheels still court the stars
high, where we suppose God wove
our need for him and one another
into seven sacraments and the greatest of these
was absolution. O shriving God dethroned by Freud
You have left us searching among the wrecks
for old wine, a Spanish crucifix,
measuring luminescence on a screen.

III *Abyss*

Wait for the head to slow, the hand to race,
the temperature of language to drop.
The light and the wind too easterly,
hard. It settles, dust, bog
the sea, its lead meniscus holding itself
flirting with the moon, dancing with the moon
fighting her with storms, not caring
about the poor life on its floor,
dark half-blind fingery things

clinging, burying themselves in the cold,
burrowing under the war. Some have survived
this before, some have not but the moon
sails and bitches, she switchbacks and rides.
The waters rise, mountains raging for her.
Houses are scattered like paper cups.
A sudden armistice. A cessation. Love reigns.
The sea mirrors her. Gazing at herself
she scarcely notices the flotsam and jetsam

Earth's tribute.
Let me never lose the horizon
defined by a tree growing up into the sky or down
as the case may be, but with roots red with blood,
rivulets of blood running into the rock
or sky, as the case may be, pulsing like hearts.
Let it attract oxygen and hold it
in its mesh of leaves, roots, branches so that
whatever the comings and goings

I can hang offerings such as bells there
and leave coins and windfall, whalebones
and nylon rope, a shoe and three cork floats
and when visibility is poor climb up
and take bearings, or down into the cathedral,
along the altar rails and rusty mineshafts
to find the cave where the handsomest drowned man

in the world lives, taking tributes in his grotto
like any roadside virgin.

The benthic layer begins at the shoreline
and drops four hundred metres
to the abyssal plane,
a jump that wakes me from a dream.

IV *Shore*

The ship, monastic in its matins and vespers
anchors me. There are no false promises.
The docks are the loveliest part of town
honest scrap, bent silver, a smelted alphabet
shining like crooked truth in the morning.
They offer no proof but the sea,
the wild goat sketched against the sky
a small assurance in his otherness
the kestrel hovering over her domain

and this handful of shells in explanation.
The poles are melting, we take love
imperfect, conditional or not at all.
The man with the injured eye
has all the names for grieving things,
I have the things themselves.
In a pause in the ship's unloading
the crew say goodbye.
We swirl back into our lives.

In the house in Seanbhaile,
a propellor churns on the hearth,
my father's chart hangs framed like a degree.
Its pencilled lines and watermarks
were my first lessons in getting away:
Daddy can we go to New Zealand or Inisnee?
Bad at geography, sea roads make sense.
For the refugee and the poor
the shore marks the start of possibility.

V   *Narthex*

High over the coral ellipse
of a courtyard in Paris
I read about Hypatia, an astronomer
said to have invented the astrolabe.
She didn't but a mob killed her with oyster shells,
gouging her until, some say
there was nothing left but her reputation.
The mob was Christian,
the Hellenistic age, ended by shellfish.

Two tramps sit drinking in the doorway.
One raises his bottle of rough wine in the streetlight.
The other takes off his holy boots and sings
Then bows up at my doorway.

History makes late sense or cohesive non-sense.
It ends in the sea and begins there.
About the Fury with writhing hair –
whether she married that saint with the flower
or why the maps are redrawn so long
after countries disappear – we hear nothing.
All I learned is that there is no sacrament of divorce
and there should be and out there, where every rock
is a republic, the sun strikes the sea floor.

I have taken a three-month veil
where a Pope studied, Jews took refuge
and GIs read out the Diocese of Tuam
and Armagh to rhyme with Parma and Guam.
O Paris, Texas, Achonry in the Fifth,
across the bridge in San Sulpice
the angel holds Jacob in perfect suspense.
Traffic begins. The heart of the city beats in me.
Something has unravelled to its end.

In the cool silence morning
spins its colours.
Lux. Lumen. Splendor.

III

What am I in for now?
Whose country have I come to this time? Rough
savages and outlaws, are they, or
godfearing people, friendly or castaways?
Odyssey, Book XIII

Veteris Vestigia Flammae

In the heart, Dido, at the breast
cradling a lifeline in the shape of a child.
Rome prevented it. Carthage
betrayed you. A child causes grief,
all kinds of trouble. Hold them twenty years
in your heart's nook keeping them dry
like bread soda, and warm. They turn
into angry strangers but
veteris vestigia flammae, we want them

and sit there in the ashes, the embers
smothered, gasping until a hand
rescues them. A couple of long breaths
and they blaze again, one more chance
to burn it all down, quietly.
It is time to let the illusionary child go,
taking the city asunder. Off your knees, Dido.

More Space than Stars

after 'Console' by Maud Cotter

Inside the studio
there was paint, plaster half baked and
a preponderence of egg yolk yellow

light primrose and the purple roses of
Irish dressers. For weeks there was little more
than white teacups from BHV

then, more sulky racehorse
than furniture, she bought or had brought
a mirror console on slim legs

half in, half out of the courtyard studio,
its hard cosmopolitan elegance
gave a wild grace to the domestic.

It cleared the threshold. The finished piece
held teacups with plaster milk
rising out of them, the many slips

between cup and lip caught in mid air
as the mirrored forelegs touched down
might be lives measured out, the sad sup
of our afternoons.

I am reminded of Mary
the Scottish queen. Her delicate throat
down which red wine was seen to run
as she drank.

Play It Again, Sam

There is a painting in a gallery in Berlin
of two men looking at the moon.
A third man stood in front of it a long time
before penning the words *en attendant*...
an Irishman enchanted by endurance.
If life had to go on and on and again on,
he found it more tolerable in France
than Dublin but English resisted him
so he wrote every play twice.

Homage

Ireland you want your fenced-in poems
cars boxed in the parking bays, someone
leaving a townhouse in the Middle-of-Nowhere
brushing flecks of meaning off his shoulders
and I could deliver them, the 01703 code
to be let in, but why? Other roads
or even 1607 would find me in France
or on Columbus Avenue, the electric rage
of translating Racine and passing the stage
where Breton tried out automatic writing.
Let me rejoin my road as she did – Phèdre.

Before Winter Comes

Huge marigolds leer from a blue jug
like tired prostitutes
with their bespoke pouts.

Autumn arranges itself.
It sets about its withering
among debris and addicts
clawing the wildcats in their veins.

The boy on the Ha'penny Bridge
with his cap out
was born like a new calf, with milk blue eyes.
Now winter waits,
its crabs ready to invade every cell
and not beautifully this year though it may
mercifully, snow.

We do not have to stay
in the wreckage of our failure
among the yellowing skeletons
if there is after all a soul,
and time to go out bravely to meet it
in sunnier places.

A lost soul might live as well in Spain
as New York, find a guide
along the 2nd Avenue sidewalks but Spain first.
Winter arranges itself differently there.
In Granada or in the grey loudness of Madrid,
it glints like knives slipping into the fug
of cigarette smoke and talk
in a café on Calle del Angel.

Brutally, they also had a civil war. Republicans
danced with the skeletons
of disinterred nuns. Fascist weaponry
smashed into poems so beautiful, Federico

because truth is the only diamond.
It flashes out more dangerous than bombs.

So now, flight. You might ask
not why the earls left
but why they never came back. We do not ask.
We are not curious. The state of us.

Exeunt earls. If leaving was an act of rescue
they left to make every moment new.
Every moment. New.

Faith

It has nothing to do with belief.
Song comes when the world is empty,
breath tight. The mouth opens to swallow the sky.

Song rises, furnishes trees, a table, some swallows
for summer, or the notion of it.
You see the tail ponds, and though you hear nothing,
taste the run-off, oxides bitter to the tongue,
silvering the line. Violets invade.

Love does little that is asked of it but this:
It drives the reluctant to the altar, to their knees,
lights candles, remembers old postures of prayer,
the fingers' lovely chapel.
Eyes lifting, saying 'please'.

Dreampoem I

In the first dream he phoned: I'd like to see you.
She woke happy. When was the last time?
Happy is a movie, a saxophone.
The second night there was a kiss, a token.

This old-fashioned courtship could go on for years.
What of the third dream? A lake, the moon
on the window an apple. Two cups on the table.
She rises and puts on a fire dress. It does not burn.
May enters and blues the world.
Someone moves in the mirror's waxed face.

Next she wakes to a missing verse
the red rain of her dream fox
gliding across the late October grass
silent but for his sharp morning cough.

Dreampoem II

As an army of houses marched dead-eyed
across the plain, annexing first Connaught,
then Hungary, then Spain,
the fat God laughed and his fat wife sang.

Interregnum

Was it in the pub afterwards I noticed you
Or was it at the well?

Six years later, an invitation to Wales.
Between saying yes and going my house unravelled.

Arrival. All undone like the night, a dress,
a life, a touch. In an hour, long ago. Elsewhere.

In a pub, by a well, between the car
and a cottage door.

You said 'Such rest. I've slept so deep,
like sliding off a cliff edge.'

I woke the other side of a river, damage done
and we were spinning, a centrifuge,

all our particles fused. Then separating like comet dust,
or flood-spoiled photographs unpeeling.

Somewhere our lives went on, the body's work
being done. The spear of your name encased

in skin festered and healed. I never voiced it.
It worked its way into my mouth

and you answered: am I what you need?
And 'yes' it seems, but we agreed elsewhere, not here.

Civet

Beset by hills and sweet water. You.
Playing with your gift in joker's fashion:
'I only got Goneril' on a Shakespearian tour.
Well, now you're Lear,
half-blind, reeking of king magic, mind still
quivering along fox-scented paths.
You favour such Eros-drenched verbs.

I was a verb once
under your tongue and you broke me
into syllables, cared nothing
for the world splintering around me.
You wrecked my house or so you tell it
and set me up in love's unsheltering tent.
I went.

Watching the Stuttering Lovers

the sky saying look, for one magnificent show
all I need is the sun over Carcassonne,
the shu-shu shock of mountains, the snow.
In one hour, can you bear it,
the sea. This is the price of love, sugarloaf,
an hour in a fast car to the water.
Can you pay it?

It is always like this in border country,
two people waving flags, planting them.
One wishes to submit to this enemy
familiar as a lover. Yet they rub them out
our borders, with a thumb. The corpses, pawns,
peasants are ploughed in, seed scattered at our feet.
Love, will we meet?

If

Love. It is simple in the end
as it is in the beginning. We forgive
the havoc in between.

Now your voice on the phone
reaches me through the instrument
of the floorboards
as Mozart does, varied, tired, physical.
I used to think I could live in it.

I mention the body. It is what we hold onto.
It does not lie. While warm,
tipsy with love it fluoresces
and the amazed heart follows it.
If you come, let it be in November.

Lie beside me like water and then
there is little more to be said,
except what are you working on,
what will I cook
and where will we go for the sun.

An Easement for the Chest

Stay me with flagons
comfort me with apples...
The Song of Songs

There is a time for knives. They glint
like eyes at every window,
a rain of blades flashing into the earth.
There is a time to put them down,

reach into a shower for one
household implement, steel, well pointed,
the one a man might hold up
to a woman's mouth

with a wedge of nougat,
and only then offering her the handle;
a time for her to eat the sweet paste
and cut a waxed lemon for his drink

and say nothing, but mix brandy,
a few herbs crushed under the blade
and reach for the honeycomb.
What are knives but tears frozen.

There is a time for honey, the comfort of apples,
ointment, spices, the staying kiss.

Instead of a Proposal

Come live with me in the house of sky,
in the house of dream and black water,
in the house of starlight and air,
of chessboard roof and seabed floor.

Be the black knight to my white horse
in the house of storm, the house of stone,
the house I made of sand and bone
for one year certain. After that, who knows?

The sun, do you see the sun glint on the tiles
Over Italy? How the body hurts, the heart bleeds
enough blood to drown a child.
Whether it's death or a love affair
God's eyes glaze. He's heard it all before.
Stay with me in the house of what is left.

No

I cannot count the parts of my heart
like loose change, coming back from a war.

You do not know what to do with me whole.
Sorrow has made you an empty well

and me homeless. Your diamond mind
cut stars into mine. Stars shine.

That is all. What do you want from me?
I have no glittering coins.

Your voice on the phone is drowning.
A hawk is hanging in the sky.

Tesseract

A cube in four dimensions has sixteen corners,
twenty-four square faces and exists in
the fevered mind of the mathematician.
Nobody has touched one with his fingers.
Nobody has sat on one or sweetened his tea,
watching it stain brown
until its thirty-two edges soften and melt
but in its progression into hyperspace
you will see a football, also in four dimensions
bounce off its endless corners and a man
moving, leaving a woman, the extremes
of their grief touching less and less and less.

Manchester

There is something magnificent in a lie like history.
It spreads, gains fashionable streets, theatres, cinemas.
There are socialists and industry. There are attendant slums
where you were born. The lie has laws,
theirs and yours; churches, one tiny, where you took
instruction and became Catholic. Like me, you said.

There is a cathedral, where you learned to climb,
to escape into the Welsh hills, as poor boys did.
There are women, enticing, scheming, over-dressed
in Edwardian verbs. All past. There are pubs presented
like bouquets, as proof. There are words of love
tears, and on the rooftops a daring boy.

There was no sacrament. The women were not lesbian,
nor evil, nor past. The city you took me to was not Manchester.
Even now, I sometimes wonder if maybe the window
where you said you slept with your grandparents
was real, and in my Catholic soul
I set a candle there, desperately, like a jewel.

Coelacanth

Darling, here is the plot, the mise-en-scène.
A man, a woman, wedding rings
the sea, mountains, action in between.
He taking what was not yet his

her caul, hidden on the land, binding,
she neither fish nor fowl, searching.
In all the stories she finds it, before diving

back to her own sort
and the myth ends there.
It does not. She is put out
and haunts the shore.

She watches him, how his fingers move,
testing the granite skin of the world delicately.
She feels no god within her.

Years have passed, Sweetheart.
Whole cities have grown between us.
We erected walls, barbed wire
for words to rest on, our carrier pigeons.

The sea warms. An ancient fish
stirs in its cold millennial sleep.
Deep in the cortex, heat registers.

You text 'I am dying.' Accusations
fall like sticks. I drop my defences.
The cities roll backwards. When, I want to ask,
when? The word smashed, like a kneecap.

IV

For he would be thinking of love
Till the stars had run away
And the shadows eaten the moon.
Ah, penny, brown penny, brown penny,
One cannot begin it too soon.

W.B. Yeats

The Lusiads

Camões, old one-eyed Man-of-the Sea is shipwrecked
holding his poems above the waves
in one hand, swimming to America
or from Africa with the other. He spoke
looking for all the world like Poseidon or Lear.
I knew his sort would never talk to me
But now he did: *Signora, throw me a rope or jump in
but for the love of God stop gaping and do something.*

Ekphrasis

This return to a once-promised place
touching north, tracing with my fingers
its alpha, beta, capa. I knew it would be in brass
the chart, not like the shield of Achilles
and shine dully under ice and by it
we would find our way home, but first
Dublin, St Petersburg, east.

Steer on by the Uncertainties.
Everyone needs America and that
is how you get there. It is something to resist,
our own interior west, wild, tamed, lost
as we fare out to see whose face
housed among the stars is released
into the soul at birth, surprised.

The Myth of Language

Hy Brasil, as described in Kerry in the eighteen-nineties
was a town with skyscrapers. The streets were lit
and people went everywhere by tram. Of course
there was water and like all such visionary places,
it floated in on the imagination, its dimensions
many. It glowed, above all else, with electricity
and remained, docked just out of sight but close enough
to reappear when the dark was too much to bear,
or someone got drunk and wouldn't shut up.

You could taste the sweet smell
of dresses, shiny, full-skirted that turned all the girls
into dolls. There were tunes, naturally, and dancing. A fiddle
playing music lonesome for the unlit roads of Dun Chaoin, full
of misery and faith. And then a slide, and the boys
winking like brigands. Said the old people. Oh yes.
Out there beyond the horizon, glowing like the *Titanic*.

Crew

after O Flatharta

It would be spurious to make comparison
with the Argonauts but they are good lads
driven to this work because of quotas
that stop them using their own boats.

They work the pulleys, winches, curious,
good-tempered, the best. Science will publish
but the poet put them higher, young, wild
as the fine cliff flowers, the sea-promised.

Thalassa

She has explorers on board. Each cabin is kitted
with rugs, a Murano vase and a small coffee pot.

They dress for dinner, raise a glass to luminescence
among the ropes and instruments.

The men, bearded, talk philosophy or mention
existentially, the havoc caused by gold and reason.

Pack the sky dress, a telescope and Baudelaire.
The captain is Penelope. Sirens beware.

Neap

First the fawn came, as real as those plastic herons
people buy to confuse live ones, a painting
with the gaze of a new child.
It was Christmas Eve, grey cold. He stood his ground

near the long window. For a second I thought
some friend had put him there for fun, I thought
the aliens have come, I need New York,
this country is closing in, and shut my eyes.

He was still there when I opened them. Yesterday the hare.
She loped towards me, swung up the hill
as if taking her country back. We wanted the seas
lavish with salmon, banked with shivering whitebait

not half-crowns in the old currency, these turncoats.
While we slept, the flow shifted. Earth's promissory notes,
deer, hare, horse and in July the wild goat
are for them, Ethan, Faith, Croia and Juliette, not us.

The Shark's Dream

There is one Lord here. Swimmers
scattered like frogs' legs do not interest him.
Perhaps he is dreaming of fat women,
mouthfuls of krill flowing through the grate
Of his teeth. His dreams are hard as glass

his fin, a lesson in the principles of abstraction,
is as sharp as an iceberg.
Its deadly beauty cuts through the unknown,
elegant as the mind of God and as indifferent.

There is a tug. A trace of blood reaches him
like the smell of coffee. Instantly
he flicks into action. What he dreamed
was that humans could make him like them
and spend the rest of his life improving him.

Caged

Liverish, stressed, drugged out, unsure
as students sapped of defiance,
they wait to be picked from the water.

Their fins and tails are webbed
from where they beat against the cage,
wearing themselves down. Force-fed

they bloat. Sea lice feast on them. Without
the pink dye they are given we would gag
at the sight of their flesh on the plate.

We know salmon tasted like knowledge,
that it burned your thumb, marked
you for life, the smallest lick
of the real thing, and hunger for it.

Cetorhinus maximus

I bask. It's what I do.
Food happens, scenery is provided.
The nets are treacherous.
Monofilament hangings,
like algae. Beautiful though.
They ghost along the floor,
tumbleweed storms.

I travel. The boats
leave me alone but sometimes
for the hell of it I flick
my tail at a twenty-eight-footer
just to see if I can still do it,
the broken fuel pipe, the tiller,
the man arcing overboard.

The Black Glacier

Down and down the divers go
two by two, ten fathoms low.

By Tusker Rock a submarine dives fast
taking trawler, crew, gear. Days later, a buoy,
a blue plastic fish box, the remains of a body.
Radio Silence. The Secrets Act.

The fishermen climb Mount Ararat,
the burning mountains of Ararat.

To All Who Are Hopeless with Birds

Fat-brushed, inky strokes of our haiku.
They denote alien calm
or glamour, move in constellations

close enough to watch with the naked eye.
What we observe
is so much softer than the stars.

We know swallow, hawk, gull
but are lost in the everyday
chatter of birds common as chairs.

Feathered, hanging out in gangs,
warm as stolen time
an hour here, a night there, snatched,

held between our hands. Yet we are hopeless,
not naming what we serve
and mutely love and understand.
Stuttering, when asked: 'Wren, linnet … finch?'

Statues

Europe is a turtle's back broken
open with bricks, with gunfire,
with love songs shifting in deep time,
borders snaking in slow motion.

My country is a worn-out thing,
badly cut and overpriced.
I only ever owned the coast,
this beautiful indented line.

It's time to shake it off, loosen
the ties, not the way some statue, Phèdre
say, or Maeve, before the nation
she wore and loved became a shroud

stepped out of it, went bare-breasted
and clothed herself in rags of light –
such get-up made the gods feel bested
its 'nothing more to lose' a threat –

but quietly, the way the people of my place
have taken boats and planes and gone
and almost always come home
for weddings, funerals and fate.

Caravaggio's Hands

Imagine. When they clean an old painting
and under the varnish the first glints
of something startling, like copper. Then a helmet
is revealed as the varnish is cleaned and faces
surface as each layer of grime is lifted. Fool's gold
they think, the restorers, hearts in their mouths.
They have been wrong before. When light
pours from the canvas, as if a new sun
is breaking through, and finally below
the tangle of past faces, below Christ and Judas
the clasped hands of Caravaggio emerge,
they know. This is how late love takes us
cautious beneath our lives layered craquelure,
an uncovering of something precious.

Homesick

Just before light it happened, one of those
dreams where your mobile phone melts
and Dali rearranges your house.
Awake, bones thin and hollowed out
from gravity, you never want to speak again.
Outside, slim women navigate the rain,
black silhouettes under streetlight
and the men too are elegant, contained
within their clothes, like Gauloises and Gitanes.

Down Rue Mouffetard the first cafés
are opening, their awnings unwound
and the wicker or metal chairs displayed
like hats. Cups steam on zinc counters.
Outside, the traffic and church bells
pulse through the arteries and cavities
of the neighbourhood, always cold
always towards the river, and mill
past flower sellers and beggars to Notre Dame.

This morning, I only want to go home
not forever, I'll come back to Paris
not, and this is the first time,
to my neglected house, but to you, my host
to warm your shoulders cold in the morning
and feel your hands mould my arms, throat,
chest, helping me into myself like a coat
then after cups of tea to go about
our separate tasks elsewhere in the house.

The Birth of Venus

So it sinks in – you are my country.
I never thought there would be
a new one with its own passport
and flag and rules of the road.
Even the traffic lights are obeyed.
We view this territory together
wary of Indians, its incomplete
history and one another's luggage.

We enter, you with compasses
and maps. I tell you, I do not believe
in their certainties (look at the fixed stars.
They wander all over the place)
and in the moon's unerring pull
towards havoc and the coast.
Only in the pattern of those birds
whose habits you read like a book

The compass, brass with the needle
quivering towards its lodestone
is soothing as a prayer wheel,
and the maps glow on screens
like pretty constellations.
We are our own cartographers.
That star dazzling in the west
looks promising. Will we name it?

Climbing the Volcano

So much between lovers happens
in the white noise of absence,
the song, the half-heard notes
the necessary arias. Then, there is
time enough. In the Luxembourg gardens
they are lifting whole beds
of flowers, a cabaret of blues.
Apart, too much may happen.

Together is clean, clear, close as Jacques
Brel singing 'Amsterdam'
or stark as Sibelius' *Finlandia*, a stand of firs
on a glacier, lung-healing green.
A lick of fire slips through it, foxes
or a torch singer's sequinned mane.
Together is a house somewhere between
those two where our familiar animals –

Do you remember the day we watched
hawks teaching their young on Cnoc a Dun
and sat until the shore silvered –
wild cat and kestrel awaiting our return
will watch the house appear again
as if by magic, room by room
where for too long dark space has been
as each lamp is lit and we move in.

The Gulls at Fastnet

Condemned to endless flight
always attracted by the ship's light

Inside I watch their eyes. A blink
makes each bird separate from the troupe
weary, wings bending the wind

in certain geometry which if decoded
might eradicate disease or at least
provide the mathematical basis for hope.

But who's interested in tired birds?
An hour ago, inches above the waves
a shoal of flying fish mimicked

them and all was silver and black-tipped
as houndstooth, lit so that those on the deck
might have been wearing 1940s frocks

Once, your lungs strove like this, each breath
such labour you wanted it to stop, just finish

the scientists smoking,
the Frenchman taking a deckchair and leaning
towards his colleague with a light

in formal black, almost touching her bare shoulder,
leaning like they did then before everything
had to be spelled out. Instead they wear

hard hats and wet gear, monitors and microscopes
everywhere. At least he is offering a light
and she is smoking. White dwarves

slo-mo across the screen. Outside a gannet dives
and creatures that want nothing to do with our affairs
veer and turn on their suspected gyres

old experts on wave dynamics.
The gulls, like silver shavings, fly on because they must
until dawn releases them, and us.

Never Merely One Albertine

According to quantum mechanics,
when a particle is faced with alternatives
it does nothing until we, human, look at it.

Then it either chooses or it splits
into multiple versions of itself whose worlds
do not interact. Our identical counterparts

see a different version of reality. Put another way,
there is no road not taken and this
makes us gods, in many-world theory.

Science is rigorous, they say, and there is
unsurprisingly argument, yet all agree
this surprising explanation fits the facts.

There is never merely one Albertine
so long as love has her in its power
and never only one soul, one madeleine,

so the quantum effect, despite unease, stays,
leaving us to weave eternally through
the universes we create, cold as theorems

hot as suns. It separates us from our doubles
who do not know us as they lie
with men we did not marry, rear the child

they didn't abort. They orbit our lives,
leave us wondering why they plunged like knives
into the swollen river at nineteen, all our selves,
heavy with consequence.

Notes

p. 26, 'Mercy': 'De Bello Gallico' refers to *Commentarii De Bello Gallico*, Julius Caesar's account of the Gallic Wars, a set text for Latin exams.

p. 35, 'Resident at Sea': 'da molte stele mi vien questa luce': 'This light that comes from many stars', from the *Divina Commedia*, *Paradiso*

p. 40, 'Oceano Nox': 'is ionann an cearnog ar an teoragain...': Euclid, 'The square on the hypotenuse is equal to ...'

p. 41, 'Oceano Nox': 'Pai / afaste de mim esse cálice', from the song 'Cálice' composed by Chico Buarque and Gilberto Gil: 'Father, take this cup from me'.

p. 49, 'Veteris Vestigia Flammae': 'the deepest desire of the heart', from the lines in Book IV of the *Aeneid* in which Dido of Carthage admits her love for Aeneas.